Risen Life

The Risen Life

JESSIE PENN-LEWIS

WHITAKER
HOUSE

THE RISEN LIFE

(Previously published as *The Climax of the Risen Life.*)

ISBN: 978-1-60374-910-7
eBook ISBN: 978-1-60374-911-4
Printed in the United States of America
© 2013 by Whitaker House

Whitaker House
1030 Hunt Valley Circle
New Kensington, PA 15068
www.whitakerhouse.com

Library of Congress Cataloging-in-Publication Data (Pending)

1 2 3 4 5 6 7 8 9 10 11   ⨃   19 18 17 16 15 14 13

CONTENTS

INTRODUCTION:

DEATH TO SIN

It is very important to clearly understand the stage of experience depicted in the following pages, for truth out of place can be poison. The title of this book is a sufficient explanation, if it is apprehended, but it may be necessary to emphasize in still plainer language that conformity to death is the climax of—not the way to—the risen life. This is the life of union with the risen Lord on the heavenly side of the cross.

Conformity to death, and bearing about in the body the dying of Jesus, is quite another aspect of the cross, that which is talked about in Romans 6. The believer's break with sin—through apprehending the death to sin of Christ as the representative Man—is to be definite and decisive. Based on God's meaning of Calvary declared in Romans 6:6, the believer is to reckon himself dead—not dying—to sin, counting upon the Spirit of God to make this reckoning true. Standing on the basis of being dead to sin, the believer finds the mastery of sin broken. He finds that he is a new creation in Christ Jesus. (See 2 Corinthians 5:17.) Joined to the Lord, he is *"one spirit with Him"* (1 Corinthians 6:17). His life is hid with Christ in God.

Now comes the question of the manifestation of that hidden life—the life of Jesus. How is it to be lived? The following pages will seek to answer this question. The truth in the rest of these pages stands steadfastly on two Scriptures: (1) *"Our old self was crucified with him so that the sinful body might be destroyed, and we*

7

might no longer be enslaved to sin" (Romans 6:6); and (2) *"So you also must consider yourselves dead to sin and alive to God in Christ Jesus"* (Romans 6:11). The believer, whose life is hidden with Christ in God, is now able to *"share [in] Christ's sufferings"* (1 Peter 4:13) and is made conformable to His death. (See Philippians 3:10.) This happens so that the life in union with the risen Lord may be manifested in the body and through the body to others. *"So death is at work in us, but life in you"* (2 Corinthians 4:12).

The need for both of these aspects of the cross to be apprehended clearly by the Lord's children, in their right order, is very important. If the believer imagines himself in the path of conformity to death when he has not first apprehended the death to sin, he will never obtain victory over sin nor have any note of victory in his life. Again, if the believer who rejoices in the truth of Romans 6—being freed from sin—does not see the succeeding stage of conformity to death for life-giving and fruit-bearing service, he is in danger of being hard and unbroken in exterior, failing to manifest the broken and contrite spirit that is so precious to God.

It is also necessary to emphasize not only the need of the believer's understanding of the two stages—the death to sin of Romans 6 and the conformity to death of Philippians 3:10—but the understanding that these two should work alongside each other in every obedient child of God. The bedrock basis of death to sin, needing the persistent "reckoning," must never be departed from. Further, the apprehension of Romans 6 must never be looked upon simply as a past landmark in the spiritual life. If this is done, sin, in more subtle forms, will reassert the mastery without being called sin at all. We must persistently stand on the bedrock of death to sin in order to enable the Spirit of God to reveal, in deeper measure, what sin is in the sight of God. This is necessary in order that, in the power of the new life, the believer does not let sin reign in his actions. (See Romans 6:12.) The acceptance of conformity to death alone permits the outflow of the life of Jesus through the mortal body, *"For while we live we are always being given up to death for Jesus' sake, so that the life of Jesus may be manifested in our mortal flesh"* (2 Corinthians 4:11). The two must go together! In relation to sin, we reckon we are dead with Christ and therefore dead to sin, living unto God in Christ Jesus; in relation to others, we accept the fellowship of Christ's sufferings and become conformable unto His death so that life may flow through us to a dying world.

Standing, then, on the basis of Romans 6, may you say amen to the message in the following pages and follow in the steps of the Lamb of Calvary.

PART I

THE CROSS

CHAPTER ONE

THE RISEN LIFE

*"I long to know Christ and the power which
is in His resurrection, and to share in His sufferings
and die even as He died."*

—Philippians 3:10 (WEY)

So wrote the "Apostle to the Gentiles" in his letter to the Philippians. Reverend Charles Fox goes into further detail about this Scripture:

The risen life culminates in "becoming conformed unto His death"; we rise that we may sink ourselves after His likeness; we are emancipated that we may surrender ourselves into the hands of our Emancipator. The climax of the risen life gravitates, strange to say, back to the cross; and when we have learnt the power of His resurrection, we are only being thereby fitted to become conformed into His death.[1]

---

1. *The Spiritual Grasp of the Epistler* by Rev. Charles A. Fox.

It is the lack of understanding Paul alludes to in Philippians 3:10 that causes many of the Lord's children to depart from God's truth. In the wisdom of God, the cross of Christ is the pivot, or central truth, which keeps all other truths in their due proportion, both in doctrine and practice. Mr. Fox pointed this out when he wrote "The cross of Calvary is the one central eminence in all Holy Writ; thither all lines of truth, whether old or new, converge, and thence all light and life power radiate forth to the universal church." If this is so, then the human mind cannot possibly grasp, to the fullest extent at one time, all the various aspects and infinite depths of what the cross of Calvary means.

When in the grace of God, by the teaching of the Holy Spirit, we have assimilated what we may have thought its fullest truth, we find we are but on the edge of a vast ocean of the unsearchable wisdom of God. Hence, it is in relation to the message of the cross that God says, *"I will exhibit the nothingness of the wisdom of the wise, and the intelligence of the intelligent I will bring to nought"* (1 Corinthians 1:19 WEY). In all truth, then, connected with the message of the cross, let us humbly recognize that even the intelligence of the intelligent is of little avail, for God's Word (see 1 Corinthians 1:18; 2:4) contains depths of wisdom which the Divine Spirit alone can reveal and mightily carry home!

The message of the cross is full of paradoxes on its experimental side and these paradoxes can only be understood as we progress in experience. There is what is called the "objective side," which means the finished work of Christ which was completed on the cross all who believe; and there is the gradual coming to understanding of this by the believer, which brings about in him the "subjective" or experimental side. Therefore, as we speak about the cross, we need to almost constantly make plain from which of these standpoints we are speaking, lest we be misunderstood. The Holy Spirit of God, we may reverently say, must be watching with tender care over the sacred message of the death of the God-man, for the cross is not a favorite theme with the wise of this world, even in the Christian Church. The very words *the cross* seem to be a stumbling block to the intellect of the natural man, even as was the case in the days of Paul. The Holy Spirit is also watching over the message as it goes forth among the people of God, for its reception and assimilation by the believer depends on the fulfillment of the ascended Lord's desires for His church. If this is true—and we know it is—that all life-power radiates forth from the cross of Calvary to the church of Christ, how much depends upon our increasing knowledge of what the Holy Ghost has to teach us about it!

On the objective side, there is first revealed to us the Crucified Lord as our Sin-Bearer. Then, all who are truly born from above can bear witness to the subjective result of their understanding of the finished work of the Lamb of God. Later on comes again the revelation of the objective fact—that in the person of the Savior, the sinner was nailed to the tree. Mr. Fox wrote that "We are identified with Christ in the cross; it is our cross as truly as His. It is our death as well as His; we have died and are dead with Him." Today, thousands of the children of God understand this and are gladly acquiescing all that it subjectively means—(1) death to sin; (2) deep separation from self (see Hebrews 4:12); (3) severance from the world, being separated unto the Redeemer as His purchased possession; and (4) victory over Satan as conquered by the Emancipator at the very hour of His outward shame!

Through this blessed work of the Spirit in the body of Christ, in a progressive unveiling of the meaning of the finished work of the Savior, the living members of the Lord's body have been steadily advancing in the divine life. Life-power has been radiating forth to the whole church of Christ. More and more, the having *"drunk of one Spirit"* (1 Corinthians 12:13) has been seen to be the characteristic of the children of God. The church has been advancing to the heavenly sphere, where she is *"blessed...with every spiritual blessing in the heavenly places"* (Ephesians 1:3); *"raised up"* with the risen Lord *"in the heavenly places"* (Ephesians 2:6) where it is God's purpose that the *"church might now be used to display to the powers and authorities in the heavenly realms the innumerable aspects of God's wisdom"* (Ephesians 3:10 WEY). All this has gloriously been coming about in increasing measure these last years. But now we ask, what is next? The climax of the risen life gravitates back to the cross. *"That I may know him and the power of his resurrection, and may share his sufferings, becoming like him in his death"* (Philippians 3:10).[2] The same keynote is struck in the apostle's second letter to the Corinthians, where he says,

> We are afflicted in every way...always carrying in the body the death of Jesus, so that the life of Jesus may also be manifested in our bodies. For while we live we are always being given up to death for Jesus' sake, so that the life of Jesus may be manifested in our mortal flesh.   (2 Corinthians 4:8, 10–11)

What is the meaning of this? Why do we need to *"always [be] carrying in the body the death of Jesus"*? Because in the body, we are open to the assaults of the world, the flesh, and the devil, while in the spirit, we are joined to the risen Lord and sit with Him in the heavenly realm. Therefore, we need to continually, in ever-deepening measure, be made conformable to His death, for it is only as we are willing "to sink ourselves after His likeness" that the true life in the spirit can be pure and grow in power.

The importance of fully understanding that conformity to the death of Christ is a process is great, for to go beyond the due

---

2. Also see Conybeare's rendering of Philippians 3:10. The chapter "Conformity to the Death of the Christ" in *The Law of Liberty in the Spiritual Life* by Rev. Evan H. Hopkins most clearly unfolds this theme.

proportion of this truth means danger in every stage of the spiritual life. Our transformation does not happen all at once. It is a process and we must see it as a process so that we continue looking to God for renewal day by day. "All truth, all light, all life radiates from the cross," wrote Mr. Fox, and if the cross is kept in its central place by every believer seeking the fullness of the Spirit, no aspect of truth will be pressed too far and no line of truth radiating from the cross will go beyond the radius of the cross.

Moreover, the fullest victory in the believer's life depends on his conformity to the death of Christ. It is the "condition", writes Mr. Hopkins, of the "manifestation of the divine life." "Our part," he says,

> ...consists in getting down [note the same thought as with Mr. Fox, "sink ourselves"] into the death of Christ; His part is to live out His own life in us....And this assimilation to the dying Christ is not an isolated act but a condition of mind ever to be maintained and to go on deepening.

This simply means that however much any of us may have understood our death with Christ as a "terminus" or "boundary line between us and the world" and as "the divine laboratory where the 'flesh' is cauterised and put to death" (C. A. Fox), there still must be a fresh and daily application of the power of the death of Christ by the working of the Holy Spirit—for the continued manifestation of the life of Jesus in actual freshness and power. While it is therefore true that we have died with Christ to sin so that we walk in newness of life in union with Him, it is also true that for the life of Jesus to be manifested, we cannot get away from the cross but must continually die again with Him every day. (See 2 Corinthians 4:10.)

It is not easy to make this important aspect of the cross clear to young believers, for it is difficult to apprehend two apparently contradictory truths at the same time. And yet in experience it becomes all so simple! "Some think that they are always to be hidden in Christ on the cross," writes a follower of Christ, but "Christ is risen, and in Him we are to walk in newness of life." Both are true, according to the texts we are considering. Second Corinthians 4:10–12 and Philippians 3:10 are passages which *follow* the experience of Romans 6 and describe the absolute necessity of keeping the truth in Romans 6 working in our lives.

The Holy Spirit has many ways of teaching these deeper depths of the cross and often uses figures of speech which the babes can apprehend (when Romans 6 and 2 Corinthians 4:10 are beyond their understanding). *"I will put you in a cleft of the rock"* (Exodus 33:22), said the Lord to Moses, and we often sing the words, "Rock of Ages, cleft for me, let me hide myself in Thee."[3] These are only the spiritual facts of the necessity of maintaining the "conformity to His death" attitude, which is rendered into figures of speech. Being planted in Christ's death, which is spoken of in Romans 6, is to be found over and over in the words of the Savior throughout the New Testament. For example, John 3:14–15 reads, *"as Moses lifted up the serpent in the wilderness, so must the Son of man be lifted up, that whoever believes in him may have eternal life."* It is, in truth, as we sink down into His death—His death on the cross—and abide in that death every hour of every day that His life—the life of Jesus Himself in us—will spring up into *"newness of life"* (Romans 6:4). Even more, it is only in the proportion that we get down into His death that we ascend into that life within the veil *"hid with Christ in God."* *"For you have died,"* said the apostle, *"and your life is hid with Christ in God"* (Colossians 3:3). Our lives are *"hid with Christ in God"* when we die to ourselves on a daily basis.

We might get a better understanding of this truth by looking at Rev. Andrew Murray's example of an acorn that dies in the

---

3 Augustus M. Toplady, "Rock of Ages," 1776.

ground, which allows the roots to develop and spring up into an oak. Christ was a seed of grain, in the language of the divine Spirit, while He hung upon the cross, liberating His life for a dying world. His death may be likened to the ground in which we are planted. It is as we abide there, as the seed dies in faith, that the roots grow deep into the ground and spring up into *"a resurrection"* (Romans 6:5.)

We might carry the picture further and say that the lack of root—or the lack of power which comes from abiding in the ground or death of Jesus—is always the cause of falling away from Christ, opening ourselves to the subtle wiles of the spiritual foes roaming at large in the spiritual world. It is as if the young oak tree becomes, all at once, all branches and leaves, growing away into space without strong roots. Or, for another example, it is as if the believer soared away into an unknown realm without seeing to the safe anchorage of daily death to self. All language fails to portray this divine reality accurately. Thanks be to God that behind all the limits of human speech, the Holy Spirit is ready to reveal the truth to needy hearts.

"By maintaining the death attitude, we liberate the life power," wrote Mr. Fox, and "the death mark is the trademark of the church." What is this but a mirror of the apostle's words: *"So death is at work in us, but life in you"* (2 Corinthians 4:12)? Here we have death said to be working! The death of Christ was not an ordinary death, for He was the God-man and His death carried power. His death is alive, it carries power, it works deliverance, it works separation, it works in the believer as he yields to it until the activity of the flesh is brought under its power in conformity to His death! Indeed, the death attitude liberates life power! Yes, the life power of Jesus which makes the man in Christ, "more 'himself,' in one sense, than he ever was before"! For "this does not destroy our individuality, but it magnifies His," wrote Mr. Fox.

The liberating of the life power—that is the need of the church! The seed of grain in the ground liberates life; the acorn in the ground, as it abides and strikes its roots downward, liberates life. Need we wonder now why, as Fox said, the "climax of the risen life gravitates to the cross"? Daily death to self is needed for (1) daily and hourly deliverance and continual separation from sin. "*The blood of Jesus his Son cleanses us from all sin*" (1 John 1:17). When we speak of the '*blood of Christ*,' we mean the life poured out, sacrificed, i.e. His death; (2) for continual separation from the sinful life of the first Adam (see 1 Corinthians 2:14), indicated in the words "*deny himself and take up his cross daily*" (Luke 9:23) and described in James 3:15 as "*soulish wisdom*"; (3) for rooting purposes, to keep the believer steadily founded on the rock; and (4) for deeper and richer and fuller liberation of life, springing upward into the heavenly sphere and outward to a dying world.

If all the members of the body of Christ will "get down" into the death of Jesus, they will find, springing forth in glorious fullness, the streams of life that the poor, dead world so sorely needs; they will find, as they hide in the death of Jesus, the safety from the enemy's workings—the safety which they need to live victoriously. For as they abide within the radius of the cross, Satan is a conquered foe.

And how can all this be? By the power of the Holy Ghost. The Spirit leads us to the cross and the cross to the Spirit! The oil must be upon the blood and upon man's flesh. "Christians too often attempt in early life to aim at being like the Crucified, and afterwards, later on, they aim at the risen life. We must bear and wear the marks of crucifixion while we, by the Spirit, walk in newness of life" (Fox).

There is much else that might be said about the practical results of death in the daily life, of the "life of Jesus manifested" in the fullest use of the faculties of reason, and our journey as we walk as He did in lowly service and ministry to all. Even so,

> *Let all of us who are mature believers cherish these thoughts; and if in any respect you think differently, that also God will make clear to you. But whatever be the point that we have already reached, let us persevere in the same course.*   (Philippians 3:15–16 WEY)

CHAPTER TWO

THE CONTINUITY OF THE CROSS

*"Always carrying in the body the death of Jesus, so that the
life of Jesus may also be manifested in our bodies. For while
we live we are always being given up to death for Jesus' sake,
so that the life of Jesus may be manifested in our mortal flesh.
So death is at work in us, but life in you."*

—2 Corinthians 4:10–12

The Keswick Convention of 1897 was opened with an address by
Dr. Moule, who spoke on the 2 Corinthians 4:10. He said that the
word used in this Scripture in the original text was not *death*, but
dying. It actually referred to the *process* of dying, the process lead-
ing up to death. Therefore, *"carrying in the body the death of Jesus"*
was the act of giving themselves up, by the grace of God, to a death
which would assent and consent to a crucifixion, in which the Lord
would be glorified in His people.

Later in the week, Mr. Hopkins spoke on the same theme.
He pointed out that (1) "the new life cannot be lived triumph-
antly until the old life is terminated"; and that (2) "it is only by the

power of Christ's death that the old life can be terminated." There is only one holy life—the life of the Lord Jesus; and only one holy death—the death of the Lord Jesus. The death of Christ is the termination of your old life. What was laid upon the Lord Jesus Christ? Your sins? Yes, and yourself. *You* were laid upon Christ when He died on the cross. That is where death takes place. That is where the great transaction was done, where this pardon was obtained, where this deliverance was secured from that old life of yours. It terminated the old, natural life.

> But we take a step further in connection with the same thought: that we need the death of Jesus every moment; we need the power of that death continually. You say, "Is it once and for all?" Well, He died once for all in the eyes of God and you died in the eyes of God with Christ once and for all. But the power, the efficacy of that death, needs to be perpetually appropriated and applied, that you may be perpetually delivered...."Always bearing about in the body the putting to death," about which we have been speaking, "of the Lord Jesus"—shall I call it the essence of the cross? It was not a dead Christ but the putting to death that took place in Him when He died—not only for sin but unto sin. There is needed the perpetual application of that to the soul—getting down into His death, being brought into conformity with His death. It is not difficult. You need not struggle or fight against the old life now, or try to tame it or conquer it or ignore it. You can claim your deliverance because it has been purchased—obtained for you by that death and your identification with it always.

> What follows? The life springs up spontaneously. "That the life also of Jesus might be made manifest in our body...." "Bearing about in the body the putting to death."

We receive death, feed upon the death, get down into the death, conform to the death....It is that which terminates the old life, which is the source of all our trouble....Let everything which belongs to the old course of life be cut off....Many of us are trying to yield the life to God before we are really cut off from the old and nothing but the perpetual application of the cross can do that....Rest upon the death of Christ on the cross.

This is just the very aspect of Calvary which the people of God need, for many understand clearly their death with Christ on Calvary. It is the perpetual application of the cross which will keep the old life behind us, which Satan effectively plays upon with subtle attacks, disguised as an angel of light. The termination of the old life by understanding our death with Christ on the cross must be followed, as Bishop Moule pointed out, by "carrying about in the body the death-process of the Lord Jesus"; or, as Mr. Hopkins so strikingly says, "by getting down into His death." The sinking down into the death of Jesus is the believer's action of faith. After we do this, the risen life of Jesus spontaneously and unconsciously springs up in gentle, silent power.

How wondrously the Spirit teaches the children of God the same thing, as illustrated by some words written by Jacob Boehme in 1622—words full of divine beauty and life. "I never desired," he wrote,

...to know anything of the divine mystery, much less understand the way to seek and fund it. I knew nothing of it, as in the condition of poor laymen in their simplicity. I sought only after the heart of Jesus Christ, that I might hide myself therein from the...violent assaults of the devil. And I besought the Lord earnestly for His Holy Spirit and His grace so that He would bless and guide me in

Him; and I resigned myself wholly to Him, that I might not live to my own will, but His, and that He might lead and direct me to the end, that I might be His child in Christ Jesus.

I can of my own ability do nothing before Thee. I wholly sink myself down into Thy wounds and death....I have no refuge in anything, only in Thy holy wounds and death I sink down....Do with me what Thou wilt....Bury me in Thy death. Break Thy judgments in me in the blood of Thy love. I wholly sink myself down in Thee. Though body and soul should this hour faint and perish, yet I will not let Thee go. Though my heart saith utterly no, no! yet the desires of my soul shall hold fast on Thy truth and neither death nor the devil shall pull me out of my Savior's wounds. Thou must, at length, be confounded in me, thou malicious devil, and thy fort of prey must be forsaken, for I will drown it in the love of Jesus—and then dwell in it if thou canst!

I beseech Thee, O Christ, Thou patient Lamb of God, grant me patience in this my way of the cross...and bring me, as a patient lamb, to Thee in Thy victory. Let me live with Thee—in Thee.

The cry to be wholly conformed to the death of the Lord Jesus, so that His own life may be manifested day by in us, is the true path of progress for the child of God. In order to understand the stories, however, from Paul's point of view, we need to read 2 Corinthians alongside the life of power described by Luke. In Acts, we see Paul baptized with the Holy Ghost (see Acts 9:17) and then sent away by God to Arabia for three years. This is where he is given the deep insight into the meaning of Christ's cross, which characterized his ministry. We read of mighty things wrought by God through His servant, but also his own experience as shown in his letter to the Corinthians. We see him ministering *"in weakness and in much fear and trembling"* (1 Corinthians 2:3) with the *"demonstration of the Spirit and of power"* (verse 4). We see him *"caught up into Paradise"* (2 Corinthians 12:3), glorying not in the visions and revelations, but in his weakness. Paul wrote to the Corinthians in *"much affliction and anguish of heart and with many tears"* (2 Corinthians 2:4), weeping over their sins before the Lord. And he commended his message by his own life, in much kindness and patience. He witnessed in weakness, suffering, patience, endurance, and gentleness—the true fruits of the power of the Holy Ghost. Dr. A. Murray once said that "The cross leads to the Spirit, and the Spirit to the cross."

Here is a glimpse into the inner life of one whom God is thus teaching, a letter from the daughter of a rector:

Two years ago I had a new vision of Calvary and what Christ achieved there. This was followed by a definite baptism of the Holy Spirit. My soul was filled with such burning love for Christ and souls like I had never known before. For years previous to this, I had been surrendered to the Lord's service and He had allowed me to win souls for His kingdom. Two years ago, a new epoch started to unfold. I resolved to know nothing but "Christ and Him crucified." The result has been a fierce conflict with the invisible powers of darkness—one that I could have never believed possible.

Misunderstanding, false judgment, envy, and strife—and that amongst Christian workers—seemed to surround me. The strain of what I passed through would have driven me from my senses had I not learned the secret of the "hiding place." In olden days, was I constantly running to the doctor for a tonic to brace up my nerves. He would just shake his head and say that I was wearing myself out, recommending me to rest, change, etc. This winter, I have not needed a tonic at all. In spite of being pressed upon all sides—and there has been keen suffering, too, at times—I know the secret of victory and my mind stays at rest. There is peace within my soul that is too deep to express. In consequence, my body stays in good health. I get restful sleep at night and one wake in the morning refreshed with renewed strength.

Perhaps these are trivial matters to mention but I find with my mind set free from harassing care and worry, I am at liberty to minister to others as never before in my life. I am learning to say along with Paul: "I am content...hardships, persecutions, and calamities; for when I am weak, then I am strong." There is grace enough for us to suffer and be kind, to pour out one's life and expect nothing in return—only that He may be glorified. Oh, the wondrous joy of it! To Him be all the praise.

This woman shows the order of spiritual progress, her growth very clearly outlined. The old life was terminated because she knew of the death and deliverance that Christ's death afforded her and she allowed the Holy Spirit to transform her soul as she continually died to herself on a daily basis. In faith, she saw the Lord create in herself a longsuffering love like that of Christ.

CHAPTER THREE

THE SACRIFICE OF THE CROSS

"He saved others; he cannot save himself!" (Matthew 27:42) were the mocking words addressed to the dying Christ as He hung on His cross on that "green hill far away."[4] These mocking words embodied the very essence of the life and death of the Son of God, the very essence of the dealings of God with the world, and the very essence of Calvary. "For God so loved the world that he gave his only Son" (John 3:16) to save others—sinners, rebels, and enemies. The Father cannot save Himself from sending forth His love through the sacrifice of His Son. To save others, the Son must pour out His soul unto death. To save others, the Holy Spirit must submit Himself to the anguish of the Son in Gethsemane.[5] He must enter into the heart of those who are deep in sin and often willfully disobey His promptings.

The words "He saved others; he cannot save himself" also embody the whole history of the God-man's journey on earth. He manifested to fallen man the "very stamp of his [the Father's] nature" (Hebrews 1:3). "In this the love of God was made manifest among us, that God sent his only Son into the world, so that we might live through

---

4. Cecil F. Alexander, "There Is a Green Hill Far Away," 1847.
5. "Do not grieve the Holy Spirit of God" (Ephesians 4:30). The word grieve is the very word used to describe the Lord's sufferings in Gethsemane.

him" (1 John 4:9). *"By this we know love, that he laid down his life for us; and we ought to lay down our lives for the brethren"* (1 John 3:16). The character of God was revealed in His Son—the divine nature was manifested in the One who walked in man's presence and gave His life for them! Here we see that it is godlike to save others instead of saving yourself.

"He saved others; he cannot save himself!" This does not mean that He did not have the power and resources to save Himself. On the contrary, He had the power but refused to use it! Saving others at no cost to oneself is within the scope of fallen creatures; but to save others and not save oneself, even when one has the power to do it—now this is divine. This Scripture says that Christ would not save Himself because it was contrary to the divine nature to save Himself at the cost of another's life.

Indeed, these are wondrous words, spoken in mockery by the lips of sinners. Even when Christ was tempted in the wilderness, He upheld this truth. He would not feed Himself merely because He could. Throughout the New Testament, we see Him drawing on the power of the Godhead to bless others, to feed others, and to save others. But when it came to Himself—nothing! He would not call on His divine resources to save Himself one moment's pang of hunger, one word less of scorn, one stroke less of the beating. Even so must the child of God be conformed to the image of the Son, to show forth His divine character, just as the Son revealed the image of the Father. *"He saved others; he cannot save himself!"* This is the law of the life of Jesus and must be the law of the life of every follower of the Lamb.

Having the power to save yourself and refusing to use it for the sake of others is what Christ expects to see in His redeemed children! To pour out your life for others, who reject and misjudge you, when you do not have to—this is Calvary! To have the power to save yourself and choose not to use it because it means loss to others—this is Calvary! To be used like Christ was to deliver souls from the power of Satan and then lie at the apparent mercy of the *"hour and the power of darkness"* (Luke 22:53)—this is Calvary!

Oh, child of God, this must be the way for you in every time of sore stress and storm. God has used you to deliver others and you are wondering, maybe, why you are not delivered from the fights and fears that are besetting your life. Others come to you in their deep need, and, with your own heart breaking, you are called upon to give out of your emptiness and loss what it seems you need for yourself. You are asked to claim victory for others in distress when it seems that you are in greater distress yourself. This is how it was at Calvary! He who had loosed others from the power of Satan was given up, as it appeared, to the full rage of the power of darkness. He who had done the mighty works of God for others laid in impotence and weakness in the hands of men. Yes, this is Calvary—life, power, blessing, deliverance for others and nothing for yourself. But, in order to be in the will of God, you must accept from the Father's hand all that He permits to come upon you.

Christ chose powerlessness, emptiness, suffering, conflict, and death for Himself. This is the hallmark of a crucified life—seen upon the heroes of faith as recorded in Hebrews 11. Among these heroes were women who were beaten to death: *"Women received their dead by resurrection. Some were tortured, refusing to accept release, that they might rise again to a better life"* (verse 35). Yes, this is the very highest mark of the spirit of the Lamb. To subdue kingdoms, obtain promises, close the mouths of lions, quench fires, escape the sword—all as the result of faith in an omnipotent God—is mighty; but Calvary is choosing to be beaten to death, all the while *"refusing to accept release."*

This is the highest path put before all those who press toward the upward calling of God in Christ Jesus at the present time. "Fresh evidence has reached me this morning that God is mightily at work to raise up and establish a people really conformed to Christ's death—a much more serious and potent matter than the granting of 'gifts,'" writes a minister of wide experience, who is in position to see and know the trend of the work of the Spirit. Yes, many tried souls will say that God is "mightily at work in [their] direction" as they think of their own case and begin to recognize the strange and special ways in which they are individually being led.

Two paths seem to be open before the church of God and each member of the body of Christ must choose which path to take. One choice is conformity to the Lamb, in which we need a divine vision to discern its heavenly beauty and glory. The other choice is the path of saving ourselves from the full extent of all that being a follower of Christ means on earth, which also means missing out on the glory of the throne of the Lamb. For it is written, *"If we endure, we shall also reign with him"* (2 Timothy 2:12). *"We suffer with him in order that we may also be glorified with him"* (Romans 8:17). The suffering of Christ was entirely voluntary, for He said, *"I lay down my life....No one takes it from me, but I lay it down of my own accord"* (John 10:17–18).

On the path of conformity to His death, many find that they could easily escape the way of the cross if they chose to. They could accept deliverance and thus save themselves. In doing so, however, they miss out on the "better resurrection." Giving ourselves for others is the calling of the Lamb, who gives His grace to redeemed sinners. All that is of the earth and all that we hear from those in the world cry, "Save thyself and us." However, the Spirit of Christ within those that follow Him cannot save themselves. To see a way of escaping suffering and choosing not to follow that way is very praiseworthy in God's eyes, for it is most like the one of whom it was mockingly said, *"He saved others; he cannot save himself!"*

CHAPTER FOUR

SONS OF THE CROSS

*"To the choirmaster: according to The
Gittith. A Psalm of the Sons of Korah."*
—Psalm 84:1

*"They go through the valley of Baca they
make it a place of springs; the early rain
also covers it with pools."*
—Psalm 84:6

Rev. C. H. Pridgeon once spoke on Psalm 84, giving some insight into the hidden truths of the passage. The preacher pointed out the suggestiveness of the address, *"Upon Gittith"* or *"concerning the wine-presses."* This signified that the psalm was probably sung at the time that the wine was being pressed out of the grapes. The words, *"A psalm for the sons of Korah,"* are equally informative, for "the word Korah is about equivalent to our word Calvary—the place of a skull. Spiritually, therefore, these 'sons of Korah' may be termed the sons of the cross." The psalm, therefore, may have been written for the use of the sons of the cross who are passing through the winepress in the Valley of Baca!

This is a psalm for the Valley of Baca, a psalm to sing in the winepress! Only sons of the cross can sing in the winepress, for they know the secret ways of God—that out of death comes life;

out of suffering, heavenly joy; out of nothingness, the very fullness of God. Therefore, they look not on winepress and the crass through eyes of loss and pain, but from the viewpoint of the Lord of Hosts, from the sanctuary of the heart of God. They can sing in the winepress when they see the wine of blessing pressed out of them to others! They know that by blessing others, they glorify the One Who trod the winepress alone for their sakes.

Psalm 84 is therefore a song to sing in the winepress! And what do they sing? *"How lovely is thy dwelling place, O LORD of hosts! My soul longs, yea, faints for the courts of the LORD; my heart and flesh sing for joy to the living God"* (Psalm 84:1–2). When earth is darkest in the winepress, this is when heaven is opened and God becomes our light. They sing—these sons of the cross—of the blessedness of the one whose strength is in God and not his circumstances or earthborn props. The Hebrew word means "might" or "endurance." Blessed is the man whose might—or power of endurance—is in Thee! *"Behold, we call those happy who were steadfast,"* writes the apostle. *"You have heard of the steadfastness of Job, and you have seen the purpose of the Lord"* (James 5:11). Yes, happy is Job that he had the strength to endure until the hour came when he was freed from captivity and he received from the Lord *"twice as much as he had before"* (Job 42:10). Likewise, at the end, we will receive from the Lord a double portion for all the pain of the winepress. The length of the time that we are able to endure in the winepress is a measure of (1) the power of endurance which the soul has in God, and (2) the foreshadowing of the double blessing that we will receive hereafter.

They go on singing; yes, they sing—these sons of the cross—when they find that in the winepress, their hearts have been *"like wax...melted within"* (Psalm 22:14). Their hearts are melted just like their Lord's was upon His cross. What a joy it is when they find that their old limitations have melted away and their once closed hearts have become *"highways to Zion"* (Psalm 84:5) for those who seek Christ. They are no longer closed to the sorrows of others, shut up in narrow bounds of sympathy and love. They have hearts enlarged and opened to the needs of a dying world, for *"any one has the world's goods and sees his brother in need, yet closes his heart against him, how does God's love abide in him?"* (1 John 3:17).

Oh, the closed hearts among the people of God! Oh, the high walls over which none can leap—walls surrounding their sympathy and love! It is worth the winepress to have the exterior of the grape bruised and broken if thereby the wine of God's love can be free to pass to a world needing more sympathy than preaching, more love than law.

Blessed is he *"in whose heart are the highways to Zion"* for a needy world—a heart open for all in need of God.

The sons of the cross can sing in the valley of the winepress because it is here that they find they have become a place of springs for the water of life to others. They might have struggled for a while, seeking God with earnest longings to be channels for *"rivers of living water"* (John 7:38), but not seeing these rivers flow through them. Then, at last, the secret was revealed by the providence of God. One day, they found themselves in the winepress valley when the rivers started flowing! It was the hour when all men seemed to trample with the grapes in the winepress of God, when lo, a spring of divine love—pure as crystal and sweet as the sweetness of heaven— opened in their hearts. That was when they realized that they were in the place of springs—the heart of God.

"If you are the Son of God, come down from the cross" (Matthew 27:40) his enemies cried. Come out of the winepress? But then how will others be saved? How will the life of God be given to the souls of men? The sons of the cross must follow the Lamb into the winepress of Calvary if they desire to give the wine of the life of Christ to a dying world.

The psalmist speaks only of passing through the winepress valley; and truth to tell, it can be only a passing through from time to time as the sons of the cross follow the Lamb. Followers of Christ are given strength for the journey and rejoice each time they are counted worthy to be given winepress joy—the joy of the Lamb, Who, on nearing His cross, said to His company of sorrowful friends, "*These things I have spoken to you, that my joy may be in you, and that your joy may be full*" (John 15:11). This was the "*joy that was set before him* [as he] *endured the cross, despising the shame*" (Hebrews 12:2). And today, this is the joy which can only be known by us through the Holy Spirit's revelation.

These souls, who know the winepress valley as a place of springs, go from "*strength to strength*" (Psalm 84:7). Yes, in New Testament language, every one of them emerges into that hidden life with Christ in God, for they are overcomers who have been lifted above all! From strength to strength they go through the winepress valleys. The more they lose their lives, the more they find what they need in God's resources. They are more and more detached from all that earth holds dear and closer to the heavens where they will one day reign with the Lord.

Being filled with the Spirit brings about this conformity to the Son of God, not signs and wonders which dazzle the eyes of men. The Lord promised the disciples that they would receive power to become martyrs. (See Acts 1:8.) This surely meant, in one aspect, that just as He offered Himself to God "*through the eternal Spirit*" (Hebrews 9:14), so all His followers would need the power of the Spirit to follow Him and be conformed to His image—the image of the Lamb.

There are two spheres of service that are linked with being filled with the Spirit. One sphere of service is characterized by mighty works, while the other is characterized by being transformed into a channel for God's life to flow into others. The one is the result of "doing," while the other is a result of suffering. The one stage may be likened to Christ's mighty works after His baptism, while the other to His life poured out at Calvary. The cross may be the "terminus" in the experience of the believer, in the sense that he dies to the world; but as he continues dying to self, that believer is led by the Spirit into fellowship with Christ and the body. This, then, characterizes the lives of the sons of the cross, who joyfully enter into fellowship with their Lord so that Christ may pour springs of life through them into other needy souls.

It is very important that we cooperate with the Spirit of God in the stage of life He has us in. It is possible to be set back in our spiritual progress by seeking an experience instead of what apostle Paul spoke in 2 Corinthians 4:10–12. The highest purpose of God for the believer is not so much to make him a powerful instrument, but to bring forth in him the fullest manifestation of Christ in every aspect of His character. And this can only be done in the valley of the winepress, which is where we suffer like Him.

We read that Christ "*was crucified in weakness*" (1 Corinthians 13:4), and that He performed no mighty signs and wonders at Calvary to thrill the multitudes. He did more for the world in weakness and suffering at Calvary than when He healed the sick and cast out demons in Galilee. Oh, that this pure and lovely pattern may be unveiled to the eager children of God who are seeking what they call "God's best." May they find that Christ's life was characterized by His lamblike humility. He conquered the hosts of darkness by submitting, not fighting. This beautiful, lamblike humility of the Lord Christ will not be wrought in us by seeing visions of Calvary, but by choosing the will of God day after day— by not objecting when accused of many things; by walking hidden and silent path of sacrifice unknown to many men; and by doing good and suffering as evildoers who are worthy of death.

CHAPTER FIVE

THE MELTED HEART OF CALVARY

"My heart is like wax,
it is melted within my breast."

—Psalm 22:14

This was Christ's confession as was foreshadowed by the psalmist in Psalm 22. This psalm was rightly named the "psalm of sobs" by Archbishop Alexander, for, he says, there is not a single complete sentence in this passage in the original Hebrew. Instead, it is made up of fragmentary sighs, like the words of a dying person when he lacks the strength to complete a sentence. At some point in the the the soul's journey, it must join in fellowship with other believers and nonbelievers. Our hearts are eventually melted with compassion for our brothers and sisters by the touch of the Holy Spirit.

"Put on then, as God's chosen ones, holy and beloved, compassion" (Colossians 3:12), writes the apostle to the Colossians. As he does in all his letters, he lays his heart so bare that he himself becomes an example of the heart of compassion that he enjoins upon his readers. He says to the Corinthians, *"Though you have countless guides in Christ, you do not have many fathers"* (1 Corinthians 4:15). This comes at a time when their faith was maturing. He lovingly admonished them and warned them to beware of the danger of pride, of glorying in spiritual experiences like they were better than others. They were wrong in glorying in material things such

as wealth and power, while he and the other apostles were living as *"men sentenced to death."* These babes in Christ, whom he could not feed with strong spiritual meat, were glorying in their wisdom, while he and Apollos were *"fools for Christ's sake."* They considered themselves strong, while the chosen vessel, who was called to suffer great things for the name of Christ, considered himself weak. They had glory, while he had only dishonor.

What a contrast between the rich, reigning, strong babes in Christ and the apostle with the great heart who calls himself their father (for he had begotten them through the gospel)! He tells the Corinthians, *"Though you have countless guides in Christ, you do not have many fathers"* (1 Corinthians 4:15). How true it is today! James talks about how there are many teachers but not many who are willing to suffer with others until they are mature. (See James 3:1.)

A heart of compassion—of yearning and tender pity—is born only in a believer that has the life of God in them, which brings power to suffer and endure for other souls. There are those who think that fellowship with Christ in His death means less sensitivity to feel, while others rebel against this thought, saying that the spiritual experience is not void of emotion. The life of the Lord Himself, as revealed in some of Paul's letters, clearly shows us the holy balance between these two extremes. Fellowship with Christ in His death simply delivers us from undue self-sensitivity, setting us free to be increasingly and acutely sensitive to all that concerns Christ and others! All that is needed to be taken away from us is surface emotionalism, so that the inner depths of our beings may be opened to the life of God.

The King James Version of Colossians 3:12 is quite suggestive on this topic: *"Put on...bowels of mercies."* This speaks of the depth, truth, and power of sacrifice which does not merely come from removing surface emotionalism. Dr. Woods Smyth highlights

Professor Bain's interpretation of Colossians 3:12, which says that "feelings" and "emotions" are "distributed throughout the nerve centers of the internal organs of the body. Hence their great power compared with mere thought, which is confined to the limited range of the head." This is talking about true emotions and feelings for others which is the deepest work of God in our being. "Thought…confined to the limited range of the head," then, can be likened to the *"countless guides in Christ"* Paul talks about. There are many guides, he says, but very few who are teaching with *"bowels of mercies."* According to Paul, many are lacking a heart of compassion. In brief, this is the heart that we want—a heart with the power to feel and that is ready to sacrifice for others. When one lacks such a heart, others interpret their advice as cold and repelling.

"My anguish, my anguish! I writhe in pain! Oh, the walls of my heart! My heart is beating wildly; I cannot keep silent" (Jeremiah 4:19), cries the prophet Jeremiah, concerning the message that he had for Israel. Jeremiah's capacity for suffering showed similarities to that of Christ's. He was a man of many sorrows. This melting of the heart—when the "nerve centers of the internal organs of the body" are so moved that the man is broken with pain—is similar to the Savior's cry when he was dying: *"My heart is like wax, it is melted within my breast"* (Psalm 22:14).

This heart of compassion mirrors the Father's heart. He sent His very own Son to visit us. This came about *"through the tender mercy of our God,"* (Luke 1:78), and Jeremiah, in fellowship with God, sees how God's heart is troubled over Ephraim—His dear son—which had turned away from Him.

It is this wondrous picture of the heart of our Father that we so desperately need to know in our own lives. When we know the heart of the Father, we can speak as Jeremiah spoke about Him to wandering souls. The Lord said, *"I am a father to Israel, and*

Ephraim is my first-born" (Jeremiah 31:9) and *"I have heard Ephraim bemoaning"* (verse 18). He also said, *"As often as I speak against him, I do remember him still"* (verse 20).

Dr. Woods Smyth points out that the phrase *"bowels of mercies"* or *"bowels of compassion"* can also be likened to the word *tenderhearted,* which is often used in the Bible. *"Be kind to one another, tenderhearted, forgiving one another, as God in Christ forgave you"* (Ephesians 4:32);*"If there is therefore any exhortation in Christ, if any consolation of love, if any fellowship of the Spirit, if any tender mercies and compassions, make full my joy, that ye be of the same mind"* (Philippians 2:1–2); *"I am sending him* [Onesimus] *back to you, sending my very heart"* (Philemon 1:12). These passages show that God enables His children to feel a measure of what He felt over lost people.

Paul said to the Ephesians, *"Be kind to one another, tenderhearted, forgiving one another, as God in Christ forgave you"* (Ephesians 4:32). Who will not better be able to tell of God's forgiveness to repentant sinners than those who have been moved by the love of God? Are they not more equipped to pour out gracious, loving, melting forgiveness to one another, even before the first trace of sorrow or regret for wrong is even seen? Oh, how tender mercies and compassion fill others with hearts of joy! These gracious, exquisite, tactful words can be found in the apostle's letter to Philemon about his runaway slave. How Paul's heart of mercy shows forth in this passage! *"I appeal to you for my child, Onesimus, whose father I have become in my imprisonment"* (Philemon 1:10), he writes. And this about a Phrygian slave! The very heart of Paul had yearned over Onesimus with bowels of mercy, so much so that he no longer saw him as a slave but a child.

What a wealth of gracious, God-given compassion we see here in Paul! Some say that his letters were written with "all heart"— not "heart" in the sense of earthly, personal affection, which loves only those who love us (see Matthew 5:46); but "heart" in the wider, fuller, richer sense, characterized by the *"bowels of compassion."* This heart is full of pity and pours out divine fullness upon all, irrespective of any thought of return. *"I seek not what is yours but you,"* the apostle writes to the Corinthians, *"for children ought not to lay up for their parents, but parents for their children. I will most gladly spend and be spent for your souls. If I love you the more, am I to be loved the less"* (2 Corinthians 12:14–15). To the Thessalonians, he writes, *"Life is for us life indeed, since you are standing fast in the Lord"* (1 Thessalonians 3:8 wey) and *"when I could no longer endure the uncertainty,* [I] *sent to know the condition of your faith"* (verse 5 wey). These verses give us an idea of the heart of compassion Paul had for those he nurtured in Christ. (See 1 Thessalonians 2:7.) He was *"like a father with his children"* (1 Thessalonians 2:1 wey).

"For though you have countless guides in Christ, you do not have many fathers. For I became your father in Christ Jesus through the gospel" (1 Corinthians 4:15). Paul says that there were countless guides, but not many fathers. Guides will teach, correct, admonish, and advise, but few will suffer for others with *"anguish of heart and with many tears"* (2 Corinthians 2:4). Few are moved with compassionate longing for others' welfare, filled with the very *"mercy of our God"* (Luke 1:78).

Would anyone dare say that the apostle's language was exaggerated? Could Paul really refer to a soul he had yearned for as if it were his "very heart?" Yes, for Paul's great heart was in fellowship with God and His Son Jesus Christ. "Desperate tides of the whole great world's anguish" were "forced through the channels of this single heart" (Meyers, "Saint Paul").

Is this heart of compassion possible for each of us? Yes, for the apostle writes, *"Put on then, as God's chosen ones, holy and beloved, compassion"* (Colossians 3:12). Why? Because *"you have put off the old nature with its practices"* (verse 9). Calvary's cross is the place of blessing. This is the place to put away the old, narrow, earth-born limitations. Let the old, selfish life fall to the wayside as you *"put on"* the *"new nature"* (Colossians 3:10). It is a place where there cannot be earthly distinctions, divisions, or separations, only Christ—all in all. In the heavenly sphere—and in the heavenly sphere alone—can one receive a heart of compassion. Only there can the soul be so taken into fellowship with Christ's sufferings that it knows, throughout its whole being, that love which is of God and not of man. It is written that the new man *"is being renewed."* This is a gradual process which follows our choice to put off all that is from the old creation, including *"anger, wrath, malice, slander, and foul talk from your mouth"* (Colossians 3:8).

In this renewal from the old man to the new man comes, in due season, real fellowship with Christ. This is when the inner being starts to be moved by the tender mercies of God, just as it was with Jeremiah when he wept over the rebellious nation. We begin to yearn for Christ to be formed in others, as with Paul; or yearn for the compassionate, gracious manifestation of God's forgiving love (see Ephesians 4:32); or yearn in heartfelt prayer for others *"with the affection of Christ Jesus"* (Philippians 1:8).

How does this yearning come about? *"He that believeth* [into] *Me"* (John 6:47, Greek translation supplied), the Lord Jesus said. He was referring to a faith in Him which opens the soul to feel what he felt, a faith which *unites* the trusting one with the Savior. *"I, when I am lifted up from the earth, will draw all men to myself. He said this to show by what death he was to die"* (John 12:32–33). The Savior on the cross draws us; the believing one is drawn *into* Him there, by the working of the divine Spirit, so that the Savior and the saved are united in His death. Thus is the believer *"planted together"* (Romans 6:5 KJV) with Him in death, or grafted (see Romans 11:24) into Him on His cross—we share a union with the Savior on the cross.

These are the stages that the Spirit brings the believer through until he reaches a place in Christ whence out of Him flows rivers of living water. The uplifted Christ draws; the believer "*believes* [into]," or is drawn into, Him on the cross. Then the Holy Spirit grafts the trusting one into a vital union with Christ, planting him ever deeper into the "*likeness of His death*" (Romans 6:5 KJV) as he abides in faith with Christ. The believer continues denying himself the pleasures of this world, becoming even more "*conformable unto His death*" (Philippians 3:10 KJV). In this ever-deepening conformity, the grafted soul, planted into Him, begins to know aspect after aspect of His death on the cross, until there comes the knowledge of His broken and melted heart. Out of the depths of the one who has "*believed* [into]" the Redeemer comes the outflow of rivers of life, breaking forth from the slain Lamb through him. Then he is "*always being given up to death for Jesus' sake, so that the life of Jesus may be manifested in* [his] *mortal flesh*" (2 Corinthians 4:11). The apostle said that "*death is at work in us, but life in you*" (verse 12). He meant that death must be at work in us in order for others to be blessed and filled with life by our works.

Out of the heart flow the "*issues of life*" (Proverbs 4:23 KJV), which is especially seen in the death of the Christ on the cross! His body was broken for us and becomes—in a strange, deep, spiritual sense—the true meat for all who are truly united to Him and live by Him, as He lived by the Father. (See John 6:55.) His soul was poured out unto death so that He might "*divide the spoil with the strong*" (Isaiah 53:12) and bring all who are united with Him out of the power of darkness. A change occurs in Christ's followers when they begin hating their old, soulish life and lay it down along with the representative Man on the cross. Out of His broken heart came the "*issues of life*" for the dying world. "*He that believeth on me, as the scripture hath said, out of his belly shall flow rivers of living water*" (John 7:38 KJV); or as the old Syriac says it, "*Out of the depths of his life shall pour torrents of living water.*" The Lord said "*rivers,*" and rivers is what He meant. Rivers of life broke out of His heart and are now issuing, in limitless measure, from the slain Lamb on the throne. The child of God must learn that only through the inlet of Calvary can the streams of life break forth through him into the world. This only happens when he is brought into deep conformity with the death of the Son.

CHAPTER SIX

THE LIFE UNION OF CALVARY

*"That he might reconcile both unto God
in one body by the cross, having slain the
enmity thereby."*
—Ephesians 2:16 (KJV)

*"His design was to unite the two sections
of humanity in Himself so as to form one
new man, thus effecting peace, and to
reconcile Jews and Gentiles in one body to
God, by means of His cross—slaying by it
their mutual enmity."*
—Ephesians 2:15–16 (WEY)

The cross is the basis of unity not only between man and God, but also between man and man. This is clearly set forth in these verses, revealing that the cross is the center from which all light and life radiate forth into the church and world. This is yet another purpose of the cross which we will now look at in more detail. *"His design was to unite"* when He, the God-man, descended from the throne to *"[become] obedient unto death, even the death on a cross"* (Philippians 2:8). Therefore, all enmity between believers and all other human beings was slain *"by means of the cross."* As the children of God, we must understand that this message is for our own deliverance.

Let us consider now the context in which the apostle spoke these words. At that time, there were *"two sections of humanity."* The first section was the circumcised. These men were set apart from other men as God's chosen people. They enjoyed the promises of the covenant and the peculiar privileges of the nation of Israel. The second section was the uncircumcised, or the Gentiles. This included all of the nations apart from God's chosen people. Despite these differences, they were both equally under the headship of the first Adam, equally cursed in the fall, and equally needy of a Savior.

The difference was mainly external, for we read that circumcision was *"made in the flesh by hands"* and that the Gentiles were *"Gentiles in the flesh"* (Ephesians 2:11). The wall of partition between them was not, therefore, inward and spiritual, but outward. Into the midst of this division upon earth, the Son of God came with the design of uniting the two sections of humanity by creating a new man in himself who would not claim sides.

To understand what this uniting through the cross means to the professing Christians of today, we must see clearly understand the difference between Jews and Gentiles. The wall of partition laid in their obedience, or lack thereof, to the commandments given to God Himself. It was, to put it in modern language, a question of conscience. The Jew strived to keep God's commandments, while the Gentile was often ignorant of God's law. In the flesh, and according to the flesh, this meant irreconcilable division. But Christ's *"design was to unite."* And the cross was the place, and the means, by which this union would to be effected.

The cross meant that a new race would be created under the headship of the second Adam—the Son of God, the God-man.

A new creation would be formed in His image. It would not be Jew nor Gentile, only sons of the living God. In following Christ, both Jew and Gentile must pick up their cross and die along with Christ. Thus, Christ would *"make in himself of twain one new man"* (Ephesians 2:15 kjv) even as it is written, *"If any one is in Christ, he is a new creation"* (2 Corinthians 5:17) and, *"It is through Him that Jews and Gentiles alike have access through one Spirit to the Father"* (Ephesians 2:18 wey).

What have these words of the apostle to do with us today? That just as it was back then, the cross is the place of unity for all peoples today. Insofar as the children of God apprehend experimentally not only the death of Christ for them, as reconciling them to God, but His taking them with Him to the cross in death, they are made a new creation, united to the risen Lord and to all others who are joined to Him in newness of life. Thus, by His cross, He slays the mutual enmity that exists between Jew and Gentile and, we might say, between Christian and Christian, who still walk according to the flesh in their religious life. The old creation, in its form of Jew or Gentile, must die to make way for the new creation, which is *"after the image of him that created him: Where there is neither Greek nor Jew, circumcision nor uncircumcision, Barbarian, Scythian, bond nor free: but Christ is all, and in all"* (Colossians 3:10–11 kjv). Or, as Paul wrote to the Galatians, *"baptized into Christ....There is neither Jew nor Greek, there is neither bond nor free, there is neither male nor female: for ye are all one in Christ Jesus"* (Galatians 3:27–28).

It is no wonder that the cross is likened to a stumbling block and its message likened to a sword or bee, for it cuts deep into the very core of the pride of the old creation. God's cure for disunion and division is not a superficial one. He is not content with the modern ideal of the union of Christendom, which practically means no union at all! Nothing but the cross will bring about the unity He desires. By means of His cross, He slays the enmity between Christians who look upon other Christians as opponents.

Accepting this truth and living it out in actual practice are two entirely different things. We are not to be hearers only, but doers of the Word. We are bound to act upon all light given to us in the Scriptures, lest we come under the Lord's rebuke of the Pharisees when he says of them: *"They say, and do not"* (Matthew 23:3 KJV). Yet we can see how this aspect of the work of Calvary—the offence of the cross—will not cease. If we are set upon implicit obedience to the way of light, faithfully living out the principles of the cross, we shall soon find the cross an offence.

The sphere where all this is possible is in Christ Jesus. This brings us again to Romans 6:3, where we see that we are *"baptized into His death."* We are *"baptized into Christ"* and *"put on Christ,"* knowing that there cannot be distinctions, divisions, disunion, prejudices, or partialities when we are in Him. How plainly the apostle urges this upon the believers of his day. By the cross, they are cut off from the world and its ways, ambitions, and plans; by the cross, they have escaped from the world's *"rudimentary notions"* of how to worship God—written rules, human injunctions and teachings (see Colossians 2:20–23 WEY); by the cross, they cease to be Jew and Gentile with opposing ordinances. The deeper we are planted into the death of the cross, the more power we will afford to the cross to sever us from all these things.

What is the purport of this message to us today? The eternal Spirit is still at work in the members of His body, urging us to *"hold...fast* [to] *the Head"* so that the whole body may increase *"with the increase of God"* (Colossians 2:19 KJV). This increase can only be brought as Christ's followers yield to the power of the cross to slay mutual enmity—that innate contrariety of the old creation which is manifested in prejudice, partiality, pride, obstinacy, and self-opinionated ways. This is when division and disunion passes away between the living members of Christ.

So what about the seemingly irreconcilable positions of disunion among the children of God? How are these breaches to be repaired? Ephesians 2 provides an answer from the spiritual standpoint. The cross is the place of unity. But what is the practical way of dealing with these breaches? Again, the message of the cross is the answer, for as we accept the cross, it manifests itself in our lives by changing our attitudes and actions toward others. So what does it look like for the spirit of the cross to manifest in those who do not know its power of slaying enmity and uniting people? How full and abundant is the material given in the written Word for those outside of the fold who desire to be conformed to His death! Believers can emulate this life to unbelievers by pouring blessing into others who will (seemingly) not be reconciled, praying for those who despitefully use them, blessing those who curse them, doing good to those who hate them, and loving their enemies. (See Luke 6:27–28.) In fact, they just need to act like Christ did when he was a Lamb in the midst of wolves, loving others despite their wrath.

This is the gist of the Sermon on the Mount. You need to embody the laws of the kingdom for both those who are in the kingdom and outside of the kingdom. This is so that you may be seen to be a child of your Father in heaven! Children of God, you are to act as He acts to those who work evil and good. *"For he makes his sun rise on the evil and on the good, and sends rain on the just and on the unjust"* (Matthew 5:45). He loved the world that was in enmity against Him and gave His best—His only begotten Son—to save the very worst. Therefore, you who are united to the risen Lord must love…Love! Not tolerate or merely endure people, but love them. Not ignore and flee from others, but love those who hate you and pray for those who persecute you. There may be a mutual enmity between those who do not know the cross but it does not have to be a *mutual* enmity between the believer and unbeliever. The cross is the answer to all. Others may call you an enemy or opponent, but the spirit of the cross can help you not open your mouth against them (see Isaiah 53:7) as you wait for God to work in the situation. "I once fled from a difficult position," wrote a follower of Christ, but "God showed me He would take me back; but those from whom I fled are still unreconciled and I have failed to put things right." Yes, the cross is the answer. There must be no enmity—only love for those who will not be reconciled. One must work faithfully, patiently, and silently, pouring out their life day by day in the spirit of the cross, until the *"coals of fire"* (Romans 12:20 KJV) have done their work and the breach is healed.

This again emphasizes the fact that the finished objective work of Christ at Calvary is never fully finished while we are on this earth. We must continually yield to the death of Christ. This includes *"bowing the head"* to the providence of God when we are misjudged, misrepresented, misunderstood, and even persecuted. This is all part of accepting the cross of Calvary. Spiritual reality is made an actual reality through practice, and how can we practice the spirit of the cross unless we are placed in circumstances which bring trials and challenges?

"His design was to unite." The devil's design is to divide! But the cross is the place of union and unity. Uniting the divided sections of humanity cost Christ His life. Let us enter into the desires of His heart. *"That they may all be one"* (John 17:21), He prayed. *"He came to unite."* Let us make His prayer our prayer. May we pray until we see all enmity pass away and we love the church like He did and we are ready to suffer the afflictions of his life. Thus shall we, in our measure, go up into the breaches (see Ezekiel 13:5) and repair our broken roads!

PART II

THE THRONE

CHAPTER SEVEN

THE PRIZE OF THE THRONE

*"He who conquers, I will grant him to
sit with me on my throne, as I myself
conquered and sat down with my Father
on his throne."*

—Revelation 3:21

These words were spoken directly by the ascended Christ and they describe the great reward that is in store for who believe. Many will ask us why we continue on in this ceaseless warfare with the forces of evil. Our answer should be to obtain the prize of the throne. In His messages to the churches, the Lord holds the incentive of a magnificent reward for His diligent followers. Paul's writings are full of references to these rewards.

Christ *"sat down at the right hand of the Majesty on high"* (Hebrews 1:3; See Hebrews 8:1; 10:12; 12:2; Acts 2:34–35) and still waits for all of His faithful followers to join Him in ruling the world.

The throne is for the overcomers! Is this possible? Are overcomers really going to share the throne of the Son of God? We can see now why, as we pass through the closing days of the age, there is such terrible conflict and why the Prince of Darkness challenges every child of God who tries to overcome. It is the testing that all must endure to reap the reward of sharing the throne with Christ, ruling and reigning with Christ.

What is the nature of Christ's rule? He rules kingdoms of the world. After he ascends to the throne, the voice from heaven will say, "*The kingdom of the world has become the kingdom of our Lord and of his Christ*" (Revelation 11:15). God "*appointed* [Christ] *the heir of all things*" (Hebrews 1:2) far back in the ages and was foreshadowed in Daniel 7:13–14.

Then Christ shares this throne with those who receive Him as a gift, who accept His grace. "*I will grant him to sit with me*" (Revelation 3:21). Paul refers to this heirship in his talk of the work of the Holy Spirit in Romans 8: "*And if children, then heirs, heirs of God and fellow heirs with Christ, provided we suffer with him*" (Romans 8:17). Daniel 7:22 says, "*The time came when the saints received the kingdom.*" The fact that Christ's coming throne is to be shared by overcomers, who are also appointed by the Father to be fellow heirs with Him Who was "*appointed the heir of all things,*" is therefore quite clear.

Another glimpses of this shared reign is seen when Paul asked, "*Do ye not know that the saints shall judge the world?...Know ye not that we shall judge angels?*" (1 Corinthians 6:2–3). What angels? Certainly not the ones in heaven. The explanation can be found in Peter 2:4: "*God did not spare the angels when they sinned.*" These fallen angels—Satan and his hierarchy of evil powers—are to be judged by those who reign with Christ on His throne. In brief, those who will judge will be the overcomers. Yes, those who overcome the world and Satan will be the judges of the fallen hosts of evil, when these overcomers finally meet up with Christ on His throne.

Obtaining the prize of the high calling—sharing the throne with Christ—was the incentive that urged Paul to count all things as loss in order to obtain the most prized possession and be willing to be made conformable to the death of Christ as the primary means for reaching such an end. (See Philippians 3:10–14.) Likewise, each believer who walks toward the prize goes by way of the cross. *"That I may know him and the power of his resurrection...becoming like him in his death, that if possible I may attain the resurrection from the dead"* (Philippians 3:10–11). In the Greek, the word *resurrection* means coming "out from among the dead." A little later in the same chapter, Paul says, *"I press on toward the goal for the prize of the upward call of God in Christ Jesus"* (verse 14).

Notice the implication of the word *if* that Paul uses in Philippians 3:11: *"If possible I may attain the resurrection from the dead."* Paul was perfectly sure that his eternal salvation was a free gift from God through the finished work of Christ. Romans 4:4, 6:23, and many other passages, make this clear but he still refers to a prize that he could not be completely sure of receiving unless he fulfilled the condition of believing. In Romans 8:17, the same *if* appears in much the same way: *"If children, then heirs, heirs of God and fellow heirs with Christ, provided we suffer with him in order that we may also be glorified with him."* Again, we read, *"If we endure, we shall also reign with him"* (2 Timothy 2:12). We shall be fellow heirs with Christ and be glorified with Him when He is given the millennial throne and is visibly ruling over the kingdoms of the world—but only *if* we are willing to follow the path He trod. He obtained eternal life as a free gift for all who believe on Him; but for His new government over the world when it has been retaken from the hand of the enemy, He must have those who have also been made perfect through suffering. (See Hebrews 2:10.)

The millennial crown and throne is in the balance for every believer, then, in the present warfare with Satan, which intensifies as the age comes to an end. The question for each of is how to hold fast to all spiritual victory hitherto obtained in order that we do not lose the crown; for we must expect Satan to challenge every one he sees moving toward the throne. In brief, he challenges the future judges of the evil hosts of darkness when he contests and hinders those who, like Paul, press on toward the goal.

Now consider the qualification for obtaining the prize of the throne. The ascended Lord tells us, *"He who conquers, I will grant him to sit with me on my throne, as I myself conquered and sat down with my Father on his throne"* (Revelation 3:21). Here we have a personal gift—*"to sit with Me"*; a personal sharing with Him—*"on My throne"*; and an opportunity to partake in Christ's own suffering—*"as I myself have conquered."* The path is made clear.

How did Christ overcome? If we carefully consider it, we shall find that Christ's overcoming had mainly to do with the world and Satan. It was not a question of victory over sin, although that is included in it; on the other hand, victory over sin is set forth in the Scriptures as the normal life of any child of God—not as the goal of the overcomer.

Christ's overcoming and victory, then, had to do with Satan and the world. He overcame Satan in the wilderness. He said to His disciples the night before His crucifixion, *"In the world ye shall have tribulation: but be of good cheer; I have overcome the world"* (John 16:33 kjv). He had overcome the world and Satan on the cross—His very last taste of sin.

Let me make this clear. We must ask ourselves the same question Paul asks, *"How can we who died to sin still live in it?"* (Romans 6:2). Our answer to this question determines the foundation that we build our lives on. The believer is never told to overcome sin; he is told to reckon, on the ground of death with Christ, that he is already dead to it. On this ground of death, he is told not to let sin reign in his life. In brief, it is to be dealt with by the attitude of death, not by overcoming. (See Colossians 3:5; Galatians 5:24, Ephesians 4:22.) The language about sin and the works of the flesh is always referenced in the Bible along with the words *put off, put away, put to death, reckon yourselves dead,* and *let not sin reign.* The attitude to sin is the attitude of separation from the things of this world by death. *"How can we who died to sin still live in it?"*

"He who conquers, I will grant him to sit with me on my throne" means more than personal victory over sin. John makes this strikingly obvious. There are two passages about the meaning of the call to overcome, which, read as from the pen of the same writer, throw much light on Revelation 3:21. One passage speaks of overcoming the world and the other of overcoming Satan. The question of victory over sin seems to be addressed in 1 John 3:9, where the apostle says that those who are *"born of God"* or have His own life in them do not practice sin as a habit. No man with God's life in him can settle with a life of perpetual sinning; it is morally impossible. However, John says that he *may* sin and God makes provision for him when he does, for in 1 John 2:1–2, He uses the word *if* in regards to our sin.

The believer therefore is not to be spending his whole life in gaining victory over sin, but understanding his position as having already died to sin. Christ has already overcome the world and Satan.

"Whatsoever is born of God overcometh the world: and this is the victory that overcometh the world, even our faith. Who is he that overcometh the world, but he that believeth that Jesus is the Son of God?" (1 John 5:4–5 KJV). This speaks entirely about overcoming the world. It does not say "whatsoever is born of God overcometh *sin:* and this is the victory that overcometh *sin,* even our faith!" In the epistles of John, Peter, and Paul, the true position of a Christian is described as an attitude of death in Christ, reckoning oneself dead to sin. He is to overcome the world by rising in the strength

of the imparted life of God—begotten of God. Satan may deceive you if this is not clear. He knows that you cannot be an overcomer of the world and his evil hosts if he can keep you preoccupied with defeating your own temper and other personal aspects of your sin. What is it, then, that we need to overcome the world?

To overcome the world, we need to conquer our circumstances, never going under them; conquer our environment by not being affected by it; conquer everything that would drag us down. It means that the victory that *"overcometh the world"* is a faith that lays hold of the living Christ—the Son of God. We overcome the world and the environment and everything that is in the world— *"the lust of the flesh and the lust of the eyes and the pride of life"* (1 John 2:16)—by the power of His might and the strength of His Spirit. He overcomes the fascinations of the world, the world spirit, and all else that opposes Him. It means the overcoming of the opposition to God in your home; the worldly atmosphere in your church; the talk of the world; the trials of the world—everything that belongs to *"this present evil age"* (Galatians 1:4).

Are you an overcomer in the things that surround you? Are you conquering everything with an indomitable faith in the living Christ? I do not ask if you are changing everything. You cannot alter things around you until they cease to affect your victory spirit. Overcoming the world means that you do not need any props whatsoever; that your faith is so rooted in the living Christ that you do not require anyone or anything to help you stand!

When God Tells You to Doubt

The second passage about overcoming, found in John's epistle, clearly addresses how to overcome Satan by testing the spirits.

> Beloved, do not believe every spirit, but test the spirits to see whether they are of God; for many false prophets have gone

out into the world. By this you know the Spirit of God: every
spirit which confesses that Jesus Christ has come in the flesh is
of God, and every spirit which does not confess Jesus is not of
God. This is the spirit of antichrist, of which you heard that it
was coming, and now it is in the world already. Little children,
you are of God, and have overcome them; for he who is in you
is greater than he who is in the world. They are of the world,
therefore what they say is of the world, and the world listens to
them. We are of God. Whoever knows God listens to us, and
he who is not of God does not listen to us. By this we know the
spirit of truth and the spirit of error.   (1 John 4:1–6)

The believer is to overcome the visible world as well as the
things in the invisible world. The apostle says to test the spirits.
This has to do with the spiritual world. But how can I do this?
you may ask. You can, at least, do the first thing this passage says:
"Do not believe every spirit." You can keep an attitude of neutrality
to all things from the spirit world until you are *sure* they are from
God, instead of keeping yourself open to everything, in the fear
of rejecting what may be of God. When God tells you to doubt,
you should doubt. You are bidden to doubt until you have proved
something's validity. Then will God be grieved if you do so?

"For many false prophets have gone out into the world." These
spirits, then, are spirits that speak and teach through men, according to what we read in 1 Timothy 4:1–4. So how should I prove
such spirits, you might ask? The apostle makes it clear that we
must test the spirits to see if they confess that Jesus is of God.

Then we reach the topic of overcoming: *"Little children, you*
are of God, and have overcome them; for he who is in you is greater
than he who is in the world." Notice the personal pronouns: "He" in
you against "he" in the world. The faith of the overcomer—faith
laying hold of the living Christ—is the principal factor when it
comes to overcoming the world and the things of the world. In the

fight against Satan, however, the factor is essentially spirit, for the conflict is spiritual. The battle is against the Spirit of God in the spirit of the believer against the spirit of Satan in the world, which penetrates and permeates the world.

The spirit of antichrist—deceiving spirits with doctrines to deceive—which the believers of John's time were told would be coming in the last days, had even been present in John's day, considering the warnings he gave the church. They were already in the world at that time but would reach their climax at the end when the overcomers would be in the last great hour of testing for the prize of the throne.

He who wants to overcome must test the spirits today, until they are proved to be of God. He must not believe every spirit that teaches through the mouths of men, however good that person may be. He should prove the origin of the teaching by considering its attitude to the Lord Jesus Christ. The spirit that is of Satan is antichrist, or against Christ, and the test given by the apostle (without going fully into it here) is manifestly connected with truth about our Savior. In the most subtle ways, evil spirits can instigate teachings of Jesus which practically annul Him and His work. They can preach *"another Jesus"* (see 2 Corinthians 11:4) than Jesus Christ, the Son of God, Who is our Savior and Lord. Beautiful teachings and sacred sentiments termed "Christian" may wholly eliminate the atoning sacrifice of Christ and be used to cover and make His sacrifice look as though it is not really needed. They who would overcome the spirit of the antichrist, which is at work in the world, must test all teaching by the written Word.

This is only one of the many ways in which Satan must be overcome in the last hour of dispensation. The fact of this warfare is the primary point I wish to emphasize. The great fight of the overcomers at the close of the age is against the works of the devil in the world, even against Satan himself as the spirit that now works behind, in, and through the world. If you were in accord with the spirit of antichrist and of the world, there would be no fight; but the very fact that you have your eyes opened to the victory of Calvary means that Satan will challenge you and stir up all the resources he has in the world against you. We are told that in the end, *"evil men and impostors will go on from bad to worse, deceivers and deceived"* (2 Timothy 3:13) and that many true children of God, out of ignorance, will become unconscious instruments for Satan to use in the day of his power. (See Matthew 24:11.)

Notice again that in order to qualify for the prize, each believer must stand alone. It that it is *"he who conquers,"* not us who conquer. Each future ruler with Christ must have individual preparation and training, and his environment and Satan's attacks upon him will be specially permitted and weighed by Christ (see 1 Corinthians 10:13) to bring about the required results. Each heir to a vast estate must be carefully trained according to his capabilities and sphere of work. (See Galatians 4:1–2.) There may be only one placed by the Head of the church where *"Satan's throne is"* (Revelation 2:13), but he must overcome or else he will lose his crown. He must not look for someone else to overcome with him or share his responsibility, for *"only one receives the prize"* (1 Corinthians 9:24). He must qualify alone for the throne, with a faith developed by trial (see 1 Peter 1:7) and a triumph over Satan through the power of the Holy Spirit.

The part of the overcomers in the conflict is mentioned in Revelation 12:11. They are in direct personal conflict with Satan now, not only with his works, for they *"overcame him because of the blood of the Lamb, and because of the word of their testimony; and they loved not their life even unto death."*

From this point let us look into the future as mentioned in Revelation 17:14, seeing Christ and the overcomers with Him as they carry out the judgment. In this Scripture, Christ is carrying out terrible consequences on His enemies who *"make war on the Lamb, and the Lamb will conquer them, for he is Lord of lords and King of kings, and those with him are called and chosen and faithful."* The saints shall judge the world; they will share in judgment. They will appear before the judgment seat, first to be judged themselves (see 2 Corinthians 5:10) and then to reign with Christ over the new earth.

"Hold Fast...that No One May Seize Your Crown"

You may say that ever since you began to testify to Satan's defeat at Calvary and pray against him, he has been attacking you. That is because he sees the prize before you. He is attacking those who will judge the fallen angels if they obtain the prize of the throne. Will you not then hold fast your crown? How are you to do it? You are to do it by walking with a steady, unswerving aim to be true to Christ and to the light He has given you at all costs. Say to yourself, "The Lord is training me for the throne." Say it again and again. *"Greater is He who is in* [me] *than he who is in the world"* (1 John 4:4 NASB). *"Hold fast what you have, so that no one may seize your crown"* (Revelation 3:11). For every bit of the conflict, there will be the gain. Paul said that *"the sufferings of this present time are not worth comparing with the glory that is to be revealed to us"* (Romans 8:18).

CHAPTER EIGHT

THE PRICE OF THE THRONE

*"Grant that these my two sons may
sit, the one on thy right hand, and the
other on the left, in thy kingdom....Jesus
answered and said, Ye know not
what ye ask."*

—Matthew 20:21–22 (KJV)

The message of union with Christ in His death, and that identifying with death is the way to the throne, is clearly set forth in the Epistles. The verse above foreshadows this. I want to press this home as a practical issue. Long before Calvary, the Lord gave a hint of what was coming. His disciples caught the vision of a throne—an earthly throne for their Master—with themselves in close association with it. Then they came to inquire Him about it. The Lord took their question and, applying it to the infinitely higher destiny of those *"who follow the Lamb wherever he goes"* (Revelation 14:4), asked, *"Are you able to drink the cup that I am to drink?"* (Matthew 20:22). Are you prepared to pay the price?

They replied, *"We are able"*; and the Lord said, *"You will drink my cup, but to sit at my right hand and at my left is not mine to grant, but it is for those for whom it has been prepared by my Father"* (Matthew 20:23). When the other disciples heard this conversation, *"they were indignant at the two brothers"* (verse 14), but the Lord called them unto Him and said, *"You know that the rulers of the Gentiles lord it over them, and their great men exercise authority over them...and whoever would be first among you must be your slave"* (verses 25–27). That is the practical outworking of our union with Christ! The way down is the way up.

Training for Rulership

There are those who will sit with Christ in His throne hereafter (see Revelation 3:21) but the preparation for that glorious day is now! We need to understand, when we know the life-union which brings us into fellowship with Him in resurrection life, that there must be an intelligent outworking of this death in us day after day. We must not solely focus on the future and how we will share the fellowship of the victory He won over the world and Satan but also on manifesting this victorious rulership in our daily lives while still on this earth. There are many references to the rulership in the Gospels and it so often appears as if that rulership is to be postponed until after judgment day—but the training for it is in this life. *"Well done, good and faithful servant; you have been faithful over a little, I will set you over much; enter into the joy of your master"* (Matthew 25:23). One will receive rulership over ten cities and another over five, each according to his own measure of faithfulness.

The rulership of the throne is not yet visible. The princes of the Gentiles still exercise earthly dominion, but Scripture says, *"It shall not be so among you"* (Mark 10:43). Now, the one who would be great must act the part of a servant; he who would be first—who would lead his brethren—must be the slave. (See verses 43–44.)

Christ requires us to become small, to be a servant—never stand-ing up for your rights. You must receive power from the Holy Spirit to submit and be a bond slave on earth, while all the while, on the heavenly side, you are being made a ruler in resurrection power.

Can you drink of the cup? Can you go down? Have you entered into union with your Lord so that you are filled with the power to go down before someone else gracefully—without being miserable about it, without struggling and fighting? Think of Christ as He washed the disciples' feet and as He stood in the judgment hall. Think of the mocking and scoffing, the scourging and beating he endured! Can you drink of the cup? Can you go down? Every time you go down, you really go up. May the Lord prepare us for the throne and make us willing for the preparation.

But I would urge upon you that the time is now—now, this present year and now, through our present circumstances. It is now that God wants to work in you. God has put you into just the place where He can fulfill your prayer and prepare you for the future. You may think that the enemy has interfered with your circumstances. Maybe they seem upside-down, almost as if you were in the devil's hand. My friend, that is God's highest vote of confidence in you! God is greater than the devil. The things that are the darkest and the most difficult—that look as if the devil was having his own way with you—make up the very condition that God can use to work out your future glory and rulership. *"This slight momentary affliction is preparing for us an eternal weight of glory"* (2 Corinthians 4:17). That is the way to rulership. How deep does your faith go? If you can stand in the midst of all that and still trust God absolutely; if you can stand unmoved through it all and say, "I believe that God is God," without any hard evidence that He is with you—then you have experienced victory. *"Be still, and know that I am God"* (Psalm 46:10). How far can you go in the dark, while still trusting God?

Can you drink of the cup? You may say, "I am able. *'I can do all things in him who strengthens me'* (Philippians 4:13)." Yes, we do know that God is able. But in order for him to work, we need to get clear away from ourselves so that we can get very close to Him. There will come a time when we have nothing left but God. These are the times when most people turn to Him and are anchored upon Him. The devil is absolutely defeated when this happens. God is permitted to work in your life. Kill this evil thing within you that wants to be something; bring it down to the cross so that wherever you are, you will know it to be the very best place you can be at that time—that no other circumstances would have suited God's purpose. God has put you in exactly the right crucible to burn up what He wants to be burnt up. Many think that victory means getting your circumstances exactly where you want them. No! True victory lies within. You experience it when, in the midst of your circumstances, the Spirit of God energizes and strengthens your spirit so that you can stand in the thick of it all and say, "God is God"— knowing that He is holding you, which is infinitely better than your best efforts of holding things together on your own.

"Servant of All"

At the end of the first chapter of Ephesians we are shown the risen Christ, sitting at God's right hand, *"Far above all principality, and power, and might, and dominion"* (Ephesians 1:21 KJV), with all things under His feet. Immediately we are told that "[He] *hath quickened us together with Christ…hath raised us up together, and made us sit together in heavenly places in Christ Jesus"* (Ephesians 2:5–6 KJV). The risen Lord calls us to a place far above our earthly lives; in spirit, we are seated with Him there. But on earth, our visible position is that of a servant for His sake. May the Holy Spirit teach us how to be, both in deed and in truth, bondservants of

Jesus Christ on this earth, for this is our preparation for sharing the throne with Christ later on.

Are you ready for this? Are you willing to drink of the cup of Christ's suffering? He drank of the cup for us so that we would be able to say in response, "Lord, I cannot of myself, but by Thy grace, I choose it." I have been reading a book written by a lady who was imprisoned in Russia during the revolution. She belonged to the old Russian nobility. I was very impressed by one thing she wrote—a tremendous lesson for God's children. She said this: "We had to prove to these Bolsheviks that people of our class could not be injured by what they did; and that what our enemies did would never make them what we are." They were sending these noble ladies to clean their floors—floors so dirty that they had to take knives to scrape the filth off—and they did it with a smile as if it did not matter to them at all. What about your class or heavenly position? We belong to the royal family of heaven and we have to show that to other people. Nothing on this earth can lower you if you choose not to lower yourself. It is not what you *do*, but who you *are*, that matters.

Paul wrote to the Corinthian Christians, "*Ye have reigned as kings without us*" (1 Corinthians 4:8 KJV). They were glorying in their spiritual privileges and knowledge, unto which the apostle sorrowfully adds, "*I would to God ye did reign.*" Their idea of life on the throne was very different from the reign of the Lamb of God and very different from the path of the apostles, who were made "*a spectacle to the world*" (verse 9) and "*fools for Christ's sake*" (verse 10). They were weak and despised among men. Yet Paul beseeches them to follow him in this path, for it is the path of spiritual power now and the way up to the throne.

"*If we endure, we shall also reign with him*" (2 Timothy 2:12). Salvation is free to all. The throne position is prepared for those who are willing to be prepared by Christ in advance: "*To sit at my right hand and at my left is not mine to grant, but it is for those for whom it has been prepared by my Father"* (Matthew 20:23). *"He who conquers, I will grant him to sit with me on my throne"* (Revelation 3:21).

CHAPTER NINE

FAR ABOVE ALL

> *"He raised him from the dead and made*
> *him sit at his right hand in the heavenly*
> *places, far above all….And [He] raised*
> *us up with him, and made us sit with him*
> *in the heavenly places in Christ Jesus."*
>
> —Ephesians 1:20–21; 2:6

Far above all." Yes, this may be the continuous experience of every child of God. However great the difficulties of life may be, our mighty Keeper is able to keep us fully at all times and in all places. Joined to the risen Lord, we may truly be kept far above our surroundings. The enemy uses our circumstances to drag us down, but Jesus can keep us far above as we learn to live in His faithfulness, cease resisting, and lie down in His will day after day, saying yes to all that comes.

"*Far above all.*" How can this be? Only by knowing God's deliverance from the life which keeps us in bondage to the things of the earth. Only by knowing the full meaning of Calvary's cross and the power the Spirit can give to us. Not only has Christ died that we might be forgiven of all our sins, but the apostle Paul also tells us that we have also died and "*were buried therefore with him by baptism into death*" (Romans 6:4).

The one condition to us being freed and living far above all is having faith *"in the working of God, who raised him from the dead"* (Colossians 2:12). First, though, we need to ask ourselves if we are honestly okay with being separated from all that holds us down, letting the Holy Spirit *"put to death the deeds of the body"* (Romans 8:13).

The Holy Ghost will bear witness to our death in the Lord Jesus if we are true in our desire to know surrender like He did and so fully prove our lives with the risen Lord.

"Far above all." If the things around us make us fret, the enemy has succeeded in pulling us down far enough to do it. *"For freedom Christ has set us free; stand fast therefore, and do not submit again to a yoke of slavery"* (Galatians 5:1). We need simply to recognize our freedom, trusting and praising our God that He can and will keep us far above all!

"Far above all." The Bible teaches us that our spirits can dwell with God, far above earthly distractions. (See Psalm 90:1; 32:7; John 6:56; 1 John 3:24.) In these verses, we see people who are able to see the King in His beauty and get such a vision of eternal realities that their earthly circumstances sink into their right place and valued at their true worth. We, too, can hide in the *"in the shelter of the Most High"* (Psalm 91:1) and have *"no evil shall befall [us], no scourge come near [our] tent[s]"* (verse 1). *"The eternal God is your dwelling place"* (Deuteronomy 33:27).

"Blessed are those who dwell in thy house" (Psalm 84:4).

"Thy protected ones" (Psalm 83:3).

"Your life is hid with Christ in God" (Colossians 3:3).

"Conceal me under the cover of his tent" (Psalm 27:5).

We hear of *"his chambers"* (Song of Solomon 1:4) and His *"banqueting house"* (Song of Solomon 2:4). We read that He "*holdest* [His people] *safe under thy shelter from the strife of tongues*" (Psalm 31:20). They are hidden "*in the day of trouble*" (Psalm 27:5). They are given "*hidden manna*" (Revelation 2:17), "*hidden wisdom*" (1 Corinthians 2:7; See Matthew 11:25), and "*treasures of darkness and the hoards in secret places*" (Isaiah 45:3). And He lets us dwell "*at ease*" (Psalm 25:13 KJV) "*in quiet resting places*" (Isaiah 32:18).

> Not a surge of worry, not a shade of care,
> Not a blast of hurry, touch the spirit there.[6]

"*Far above all.*" When we are far above all, we know that God will use all our circumstances to shape us for His good. Here we can reverently say with Jesus, "*Shall I not drink the cup which the Father has given me?*" (John 18:11). (Notwithstanding that the cup of sorrow came from the hand of Judas). Misunderstanding, sorrows, and trials may come, but the one who lives far above all yearns to follow, in his earthward life, the footsteps of Christ in His gentleness, meekness, lowliness, and love. When we live far above all with God, we can rejoice in our call to be a servant.

"*Do you believe that I am able to do this?*" They said to him, "*Yes, Lord.*"   (Matthew 9:28)

---

6. Frances R. Havergal, "Like a River Glorious," 1876.

ABOUT THE AUTHOR

Jessie Penn-Lewis (1861–1927) was an evangelist and author from England. Evan Roberts, who was instrumental in the Welsh revival in the early 1900s, stayed with Mrs. Penn-Lewis and her husband, William, for a time. Mrs. Penn-Lewis had been an eye-witness to the revival. Her book *War on the Saints*, which Roberts contributed to, was written to counter what she perceived as the excesses of the revival and the deceptions of Satan at work to prevent the true work of God in awakening. It is still considered a textbook on spiritual warfare by many Christians. Mrs. Penn-Lewis also established and edited the periodical *The Overcomer*.